Contents

Preface 2

Disruption and the Digital World 6

The Evolution of Marketing 9

Affiliate Marketing Platforms 15

The Journey to Success 18

Step 1: Idea Generation 20

Step 2: Creation and Design 24

Step 3: Marketing and Selling 37

Step 4: Growing and Leveraging 41

Summary 44

Becoming an Affiliate 46

Useful Tools and Links 49

Disclaimer 51

Preface

First of all, I'd like to personally congratulate you on purchasing this book as this symbolises your first step towards building a secondary income via the digital world. It is very important that you are serious about learning how to make money online as this is not something that will happen overnight (although, as you read on, you will be pleased to find out how quickly and easily you can make your first sale). The reason I decided to write this book was very simple. When I was exploring methods to generate a secondary income online, with my limited skillset, budget, and availability of time, I struggled to find anything that honestly and directly educated and guided me. Through various web searches, I came across multitudes of websites, individuals, services, and books promising the world but ultimately failing to deliver anything. I've spent my fair share of money on products online that simply have not delivered what was promised and I am absolutely sure that I am not the only one who has fallen victim to this.

With that in mind, the purpose of this book is to clearly and honestly provide you with relevant information and guidance on how you can generate an income online, suggest multiple approaches that you can tailor based on your own personal preferences, and give you a step-by-step guide to getting started. This will hopefully mean that you will earn your first dollar and eventually your first $10,000 in less time than it took me (under 6 months)!

Due to the lack of simple and honest articles and products available on the web, I learnt how to generate a secondary income online the hard way, by simply giving it a shot and learning through the process. Like most of you, I have a job, I work hard, and I'm proud to say that I am good at what I do. However, I have ambitions beyond my job and have always striven to identify additional opportunities to generate income, ideally while doing something I enjoy. Like most people, I did not have the luxury of lots of spare time or money which meant traditional income generating options were not suitable. I did not have the time or motivation to get a second job and I did not have enough cash or knowledge to confidently invest in stocks, bond, real estate etc. This meant I had to think outside the box and find a way to generate a second income with both limited time and money.

I've always had an interest in sports betting and tend to place a bet every now and again. If you are against gambling or don't see where I am going with this, please read on as I promise there is a very important point I'm looking to make. I'm a very calculated punter and very rarely (if ever) place bets on impulse. Through several years of betting on sports (primarily football AKA soccer) and trying out multiple approaches and strategies, I've managed to devise several which tend to consistently generate profits over time. In my efforts to devise profit making strategies, I did a lot of research online and came across several products on the web which promised a sizeable income through betting. I noticed that most of these products were being created and sold online by regular people via an online affiliate marketing platform. While it was nice to generate a small income on the side through my betting initiatives, it was always purely a hobby and was not something I wanted to rely on to generate a secondary income from as it lacks consistency, is risky, and would simply take the fun out of it if I relied on it for a steady income.

With this in mind, I spotted an opportunity. The majority of the betting products or services I came across seemed to lack honesty, transparency, customer service and at times, came across as scams. I thought to myself, with my betting experience and the strategies that I have managed to devise, improve and perfect over time, why not create a service of my own, sharing the knowledge I have gathered, while focusing on a genuine customer experience. If individuals on the web believe in my strategy and appreciate my direct/honest approach, it will sell, and if not, then I wouldn't be losing anything and would learn something from the process. I would simply have to invest a bit of time in documenting the strategy (which was relatively easy as it was second nature to me), purchase a domain (around $30), and build a very simply website/sales page (I used a basic drag and drop builder). Long story short, the service has surpassed my expectations and I managed to earn my first $10,000 within the first 6 months.

While this might not sound like a lot of money to some, it has been a game changer for me and has presented several additional opportunities for me, which I plan to explore over the next few years. Hopefully at that point, I will have published my next book…"My first $50,000" or maybe even "My first $100,000". The point of the story above was to highlight that I generated $10,000, in a short space of time, by simply doing something that I already did as a hobby. Everyone has something they are passionate about, interested in, or skilled at which means that everyone has the opportunity to do what I have done. If you are motivated to make money and are passionate about ANYTHING (cooking, traveling, gardening, sewing, gambling, investing, building, running, swimming…the options are endless) then I highly recommend that you continue reading as I will spell out for you the steps that you can take and the options that are available for you to make your first $10,000.

Before jumping into the details, I'd like to re-emphasize that the purpose of this book is to guide you on creating a SECONDARY income online. Unlike several other publications, I am not falsely going to promise you six figures with minimal effort. This will take some time and some effort, and will hopefully result in you generating a secondary income doing something you are passionate about, while creating additional opportunities to further grow your income and maybe even make a career out of it. I truly hope this can be the start of something big for you and wish you the best of luck!

Disruption and the Digital World

The world is changing quicker and more frequently than ever before, in literally every aspect, and the key driver behind the majority of change is technology. The introduction of the internet and email followed by social media and mobile applications has resulted in significant disruption to the way things are traditionally done, and organisations who have failed to react have faced dramatic downfalls that very few would have predicted.

HMV, the dominating figure in the music sales industry enjoyed massive success selling music in the form of records, audio cassettes and CDs. However, since the rise of the internet, the popularity of online music streaming services and the purchasing of music online (MP3s) has quickly increased. HMV however continued to focus on selling music via the traditional channels and failed to react quickly enough to the changing market. As a result, HMV, one of the largest music sales companies went into administration and is now being rescued to ensure it does not completely disappear.

Similarly, Nokia dominated the mobile phone industry for a long time and its phones, games, and new product launches were highly anticipated to the envy of its struggling competitors. However, with the introduction of touch screen technology, Apple took a calculated risk and created a purely touch screen based phone which was very positively received by the market. Nokia however continued to focus on its traditional cell phone design and by the time they decided to react, the market was flooded with touch screen phones designed and sold by a growing list of competitors (Apple,

Samsung, LG, HTC, etc.). Now, although still present in the cell phone market, Nokia is a small player that has fallen far behind and has lost a large, previously loyal customer base, while Apple's valuation has grown larger than the GDPs of several countries.

The changing digital world has created several opportunities for new companies to emerge while those who are slow to react, very quickly fall behind the pack. More and more people, of all ages are embracing technology which means it is a rapidly growing market and with endless opportunities. There are more people online now than ever before, and the number is only rising each and every day. Ultimately, anyone without an online presence is losing out on endless exposure.

Traditionally, if someone wanted to sell something, they would set up a shop, hire a shop keeper, and have set hours of operation. This meant that they had to pay to set up/design the shop, pay rent for the space, pay for the utilities, pay for the labor, and possibly pay for additional space to store their inventory. In addition to the cost involved, all of this would take lots of time to set up and they would only be able to sell during their operating hours to individuals who physically visit their shop and decide to purchase something.

With the introduction of the internet, e-commerce and web stores are becoming the new norm and the reasons are very obvious. The costs are significantly lower, it all takes far less time, and the exposure is exponentially higher. Anyone who wants to sell something now can simply purchase a domain and have a web store built within hours, without any expert knowledge. Previously, a web developer would have been required to create a website and build a web store. However, the introduction of drag and drop builders and dedicated services mean that anyone, however technical or non-technical, can very quickly and easily have a website up and running in a VERY short space of time. In addition, a website, unlike a physical store, runs 24 hours a day 7 days a week, is automated and is accessible by anyone around the world. This means, you could literally be making sales in your sleep.

The key point here is that the effort required to set up a store and begin selling something is significantly lower today than it has ever been in the past and the number of buyers in the market are larger than ever before. Therefore, trying to sell something online is far less risky and is a far smaller commitment, but can generate significant revenue due to the high margins and sales volumes that can be obtained.

The Evolution of Marketing

One of the key questions or concerns that will stem from all my previous points is marketing. I've highlighted multiple benefits that the digital world has introduced and several reasons selling online is a huge opportunity for everyone. However, what this also means is that the due to the ease of being able to sell online, the market is flooded with lots of products, services, and content that are of varying quality. What tends to set a good product apart from a bad product is the ability that it has to market itself.

Traditionally, if someone is selling something in a physical shop, one of their primary concerns is to ensure people visit their store and ultimately buy their product. In order to do this, they would use traditional marketing channels such as radio, magazine, or TV ads, flyers, billboards, trade fairs, word of mouth, an attractive shop window etc. Again, while several of these methods are effective, they tend to be very expensive and in most cases are only used by companies with large budgets. Additionally, it can be very hard to track the actual value that each marketing campaign is generating. For example, paying for a billboard ad campaign in a subway station may result in great exposure. However, there is no convenient way for the company to know how many people visited their store or purchased their product as a result of viewing that subway ad. As a result, an expensive marketing campaign can be a bit of a gamble as it may or may not generate the traffic and sales that you require.

In the digital world, there are several new methods of marketing available to sellers which are far cheaper and much more measurable. There are multiple options available to market a product or service including banner ads (pay per click), article marketing, email marketing, social media marketing, affiliate marketing, etc. Similar to traditional means, a seller can post an ad on the internet and pay for the ad space based on the number of users that actually click on the ad. This means that the seller is only paying for the value that the ad generates and can track exactly how effective the ad was, who responded to the ad, from which parts of the world, at what times, etc. Similarly, articles can be written about a seller's product to help increase exposure, targeted emails can be sent to users about products, and products can be marketed via social media channels such as Facebook, Twitter, Vine, YouTube, etc.

The key method of marketing however, that I would like to focus on in this book is affiliate marketing. Affiliate marketing seems to be one of the least talked about methods of marketing, but in my opinion, is one of the most, if not the most effective. Simply put, affiliate marketing is where an affiliate (or a third party) is used to help promote a product or service, and in return receives some form of commission, revenue share, or compensation for their efforts. The internet is full of very powerful and influential individuals or sources who can mean the difference between success and failure. These potential affiliates come in the form of bloggers, article authors, YouTubers, and email marketers who tend to have large followings of (loyal) users who frequently engage with their content and are highly influenced by these affiliates.

Let's use fitness as an example: There are lots and lots of individuals who blog and write articles online about fitness, staying in shape, nutrition, work-out regimes, etc. Many of them have followings of users in the thousands to the millions who frequently visit their website(s) and read/engage with their content. Additionally, several of them are subscribed to the blogger's mailing list(s) and frequently receive and read emails sent directly from the blogger to the individuals. None of these powerful and influential bloggers simply post content for free with no income stream in mind, and are generally very calculated in their approaches to ensure that their users remain loyal, engaged, and keep coming back for more.

Let's say that you are passionate about fitness and are interested in creating your own work-out regime (e.g. a workout guide or a workout video) and nutritional guide (what to eat, when, etc.). This is something that you have an interest in and something that you already do. You record your workout video(s) and put together a short guide on nutrition containing some information on calorie counting and eating several small meals a day. Now that your product is ready, you are excited to begin selling it but have no idea where and how to start marketing. One option could to be market your product via the methods I initially highlighted and to post some pay-per-click ads and social media ads, with the hope that the users who are directed to your product will purchase it. This is one legitimate way of marketing online but is far less predictable, can be costly, can take time, and may not result in any sales as the marketing is not specifically targeted at the kind of users you necessarily want to focus on.

Another option would be to market your product via an affiliate marketing platform (will go into further detail on platforms later in this book as I don't want it to distract you from the key points I'm trying to communicate here). As previously mentioned, we can assume that affiliates already have significant followings of loyal users. You can post your new fitness product on the affiliate marketing platform and offer a pre-set commission (e.g. 50%) based on each sale that is generated. What this essentially means is that any affiliate that chooses to promote your product will receive 50% commission of any sale that they generate. The higher the commission, the more affiliates you are likely to attract as they are looking to make money. At the same time, a high quality product can also contribute to attracting affiliates.

Once you list your product along with the offered commission on the affiliate marketing platform, affiliates will begin promoting it if it is of interest to their user base and if the product and/or the commission are appealing. One post about your new product by a fitness blogger who has a readership of 100,000 users could result in exposure, traffic, and a wave of sales far larger than you would have ever generated via pay-per-click or social media advertising. Let's assume that 50,000 of the 100,000 users read the blog post about your product. From the 50,000 who read it, 10% of them (5000 users) click on the link to your product website/sales page. Of the 5000 users who land on your website, let's assume that 2% of them (100 users) purchase your product. If your product is priced at $20, you will have generated $2000. Even if you paid out 50% in commissions, you will have made a cool $1000 from a simple post by an influential affiliate. If ten affiliates write articles, send emails, or post blogs about your product, the traffic, sales, and revenue will quickly multiply.

The key take away is that with affiliate marketing, you only pay out a commission when a sale is made. Therefore, if there are no sales, then your commission pay-outs are zero and if there are sales, then you are making money. The other key point is that unlike other forms of marketing, your product will be marketed specifically to individuals who are interested in it as affiliates will only market your product if they believe it is suitable for their user base (e.g. an affiliate blogs about your fitness product on their fitness blog). Here is a quick comparative example to demonstrate the role affiliates play both in the digital and in the non-digital world:

> *You design a new clothing line and are excited to begin selling. However, your brand lacks credibility, history, or an identity. In order to begin gaining exposure and traffic, you consider two options:*
>
> ***Option 1*** *is to set aside a significant budget and to run some TV and magazine ads to help create buzz around your clothing line. At the same time, you will open stores that are dedicated to your clothing line and hire employees to run those stores.*
>
> ***Option 2*** *is to approach several existing department stores, which already have a loyal customer base and a reputable image and to offer them the opportunity to sell your clothing line in their store for a share of the revenue.*

To me, the choice is a no brainer. If you do not have a large budget or lots of time and your goal is to begin making money as soon as possible, option 2 is the way to go. Option 2 provides you with instant traffic and endorsement from reputable department stores, which will essentially act as your affiliates and will take a share of the revenue that your clothing line generates.

Similarly in the digital world, if you were launching a new clothing line, your options would be to create your own web store and to spend money on marketing your website online to begin generating traffic. Alternatively, you could simply create your web store and leave the marketing to a set of reputable affiliates who can direct traffic to your website for a share of the revenue. Once again, unless you have the luxury of a large budget and a sizeable online presence, the smart route would be to leave the hard work to the affiliates.

I hope the simple examples above helped demonstrate the power behind affiliate marketing and the amount of revenue or money that you can generate by creating a product that you are passionate about and how that can take you closer to making your first $10,000.

Affiliate Marketing Platforms

Now that you have a high level understanding of the digital landscape and affiliate marketing, let's dive into a bit more detail on the role that affiliate marketing platforms play. Affiliate marketing platforms offer lots of functionality and features that help connect creators of products/services with affiliates who have the influence to effectively market and sell these products. The descriptions below should help simplify the roles that creators and affiliates play:

1. **Creators:** *Affiliate marketing platforms allow creators to list products or services they have created on the platform's marketplace. Some platforms also offer services to help creators build sales pages and web stores for their products/services. This officially makes the product/service available for affiliates to begin marketing. The platforms also provide creators with a facility to collect/process payments for their product/service (via multiple payment methods and multiple currencies) and will automatically manage commission payments to affiliates based on the agreed commission structure. Additionally, these platforms track and report lots of valuable information such as the amount of traffic your product/service is receiving, the amount of traffic each affiliate is generating, your sales and commission figures, your popularity against other competing products, and your cancellation/refund rates. This provides creators with a complete package of features that will allow them to easily build and list their product, generate traffic, and begin selling.*

2. **Affiliates:** *Affiliate marketing platforms allow affiliates to browse through their marketplace to identify products which are*

suitable to market to their followers. Information on the products such as their popularity, the commission being offered, and the refund rate are made available to help the affiliates judge the quality of the products. Once an affiliate selects the products they would like to market, a unique link is instantly generated by the platform for the affiliate. The affiliate simply has to use the unique link to direct traffic to the product sales page and the platform will ensure that the affiliate is paid the appropriate commission for any resulting sales. The affiliate can also track which products are converting the best to ensure they only continue to market products that will generate a commission. This provides affiliates with the perfect place to identify suitable products, share them with their followers, and collect any resulting commissions.

There are several affiliate marketing platforms which provide the features highlighted above such as ClickBank, ClickSure, BlueSnap, Commission Junction, clickbooth, MaxBounty, PeerFly, and ShareASale. However, as I generated my first $10,000 with ClickBank, this book will focus on them. ClickBank is widely known to be the largest and easiest affiliate marketing platform to use and my experience selling products on their platform has been very positive. CB offers all the features discussed above (and more) and is used by lots of very powerful "super" affiliates who can generate lots of traffic and sales for your products. CB has served as the vehicle to my success and hopefully can take you on a similar journey.

Author's Advice: *My advice would be to <u>create an account with ClickBank</u> and to begin browsing through the website to get a feel for the interface and the features that are available. At this stage, do not worry about creating anything or setting anything up, but familiarising yourself* *with the platform can make the rest of the book a lot easier to digest and it will help to kick start your creativity.*

The Journey to Success

The purpose of the sections you have read so far were primarily to give you enough background information on the digital landscape so that you can easily digest and apply the information provided in the rest of the book. Next, I'll focus on the actual steps that you should take to begin brainstorming, building, marketing, selling, and leveraging your own product/service via ClickBank.

Note: *You can apply the same principles for all affiliate marketing platforms, but the specific examples used throughout the rest of the book will focus on ClickBank's platform and interface.*

When I embarked on my journey to identifying, creating, and selling my first product, it was a winding road with lots of speedbumps, dead ends, and U-turns. Looking back on my journey and accounting for all my learnings, I've summarised the process for you into 4 key steps which are explained in detail throughout the rest of the book.

The four steps above may seem over simplified and obvious, which they probably are. However, far too often, due to varying factors such as impatience and lack of experience, each of the steps aren't given the right amount of focus and dedication and as a result, the end product isn't as successful as it can and should be. The purpose of the model above is to ensure that, as you embark on your journey, you give each step the respect that it deserves which will help improve the chances of success and the speed at which you can earn your first $10,000.

Author's Advice: *At this stage, I highly recommend that you make a personal commitment to give each step the attention it deserves and to avoid "short-cuts" to quickly bring a product to market. As you continue reading, try your best to apply all the instructions and advice to help improve the quality of your product/service and ultimately your chances of success.*

Step 1: Idea Generation

At the start of the book I mentioned that everyone is passionate about, interested in, or skilled at something. My journey to my first $10,000 began with me identifying something I enjoy doing and finding a way to package it into a product/service that would appeal to others with the same interests. I noticed that I frequently bet on football matches as a hobby and that I had generated a wealth of knowledge that could benefit others who lack the experience that I have had with betting. Naturally, as I learnt about affiliate marketing, that was the niche I decided to target.

This is a very important step in the process, if not the most important. Coming up with an idea and focusing on a niche is not just about identifying something that you think will sell, but instead thinking of something that you enjoy doing, are good at, or are interested in. In the long run, if you identify something that you personally enjoy, you will be far more likely to turn it into something sustainable, scalable, and successful. Take a few minutes, a few hours, or a few days to answer the following questions:

- What are my hobbies?
- What do I enjoy doing in my free time?
- What is something I am skilled at?
- What valuable knowledge or experience do I have that others can benefit from?
- What do people often say I am good at?
- What is the first thing people think of when they think of me?
- What am I interested in learning more about?

Once you answer the questions above, try to identify common themes. Have you mentioned a specific activity, skill, or interest multiple times? Have others noticed the same thing about you as well? For example, let's say you notice that cooking is a common theme within your answers and that friends/family think you are a great cook, and cooking is something you personally enjoy. Take that interest and try to dig a bit deeper. What is it about cooking that you are good at? Are you a good baker? Are you good at or interested in cooking a specific cuisine? Do you focus on cooking a specific type of meal (breakfast, lunch, dinner)? Do you have specific medical or dietary requirements that your meals revolve around (gluten free, sugar free, vegan, etc.).

After digging a bit deeper, let's say you noticed that you tend to cook a lot of Italian food and that most of your meals take less than 30 minutes to cook. You have just successfully identified a category (cooking) and a niche (quick Italian meals).

Go through this same exercise with all the interests that stand out to you and all the common themes you identify until you find something that you are happy with.

Author's Advice: *If you struggle to identify a subject, visit* <u>DMOZ</u> *and browse through the categories to help pick a niche. I would highly recommend picking something specific (e.g. Health → Beauty → Hair) versus something generic (e.g. Health). The reason for this is that it is a lot easier to design a product and target a market segment with a specific topic/niche. Keeping things broad makes it harder to differentiate yourself and will mean that you need a far more comprehensive product/service which is hard to do as an individual with limited time and money.*

Alternatively, I would suggest visiting the ClickBank Marketplace *for inspiration. The CB Marketplace lists out all the products that are currently being sold on ClickBank and also breaks them down into several categories and sub categories. Browsing through the categories and through the products that are being sold can quickly help you identify a niche and an idea that works for you. When I was going through this process, I navigated to the "Betting Systems" category within the CB marketplace and realised that there were very few products being sold in the "Soccer" category as compared to other sports such as "Horse Racing". This helped increase my confidence in my idea as competition was slim and I would be filling a gap in the market. The screenshot below provides you information and guidance on how to navigate through the CB marketplace.*

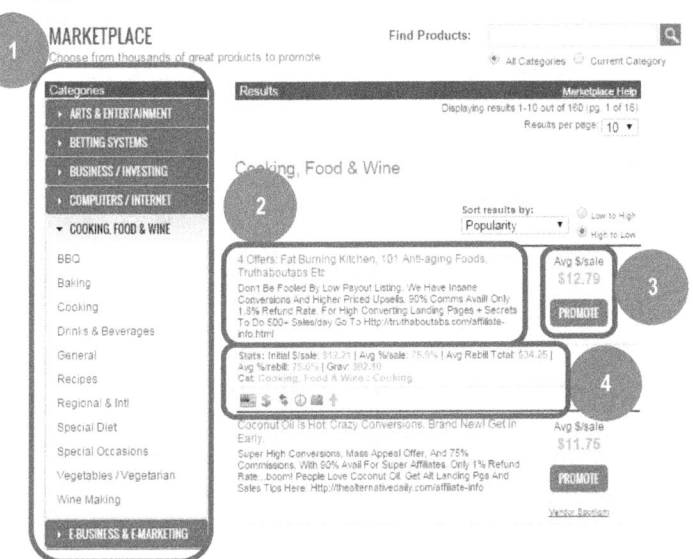

1	You can browse through the categories and sub categories using the left panel in the CB marketplace
2	You can view a description of the products in the marketplace
3	You can view the average commission that is generated by each sale of the product
4	You can view valuable information such as the commission % offered, the language of the product, and the popularity of the product.

Once you come up with an idea/niche (or a few ideas/niches), it's time to move on to step 2 which will focus on creating and designing your product/service.

Step 2: Creation and Design

Personally, I believe that the hardest part in the journey to success is step 1, do not hesitate to spend lots of time on it. Once you have identified a niche or have selected a topic that you are happy to proceed with, it is time to begin designing and creating your product.

Step 2 for me is the most fun step of the process as it allows you to get creative and build something from nothing, which can be very rewarding. There are two key aspects of creation and design that need to be covered before you can proceed to step 3. Firstly, you need to create the product/service that you are looking to sell. Secondly, you need to create an online presence from where you can begin selling your product. Let's examine the two items a step at a time.

Creating Your Product/Service

As I mentioned, you've completed the hard part and have selected a niche that you want your product/service to revolve around. Your next step is to actually design and create the product/service itself. Before jumping into the specifics, take a step back and think about what sort of product you are interested in creating.

In the digital world, there are multiple approaches you can take when building a product/service. Here are some of the most popular options:

- E-books
- Video tutorials/guides
- Email subscription services

- Bespoke/customized services

One of the key benefits of all of the items above is that they are all digital products. What this essentially means, is that unlike traditional "physical" products, they do not require manufacturing and storage. As a result, most of the effort is spent building the initial product and the ongoing costs/effort of distributing and selling the product/service are extremely low. Let's examine each of the options above in a bit more detail:

E-books: From all the options listed above, e-books are probably the most popular of all. The reason behind this is that most people have knowledge that they want to share to help benefit others and the best way of doing this is usually to document it on paper. The primary benefit of writing an e-book is that you only have to write it once, and once written, it is available to sell for the rest of your life. If it proves popular, something that took you a few hours or days to write could end up generating an income for months or years. As it is a digital product ("electronic" book), there is no printing, publishing, or storing involved and the only cost is the time you spend writing and designing it. Additionally, e-books are suitable for any niche as you simply have to record the knowledge you have into an electronic document. The only downside of an e-book is that you can only make one sale per customer and that there is no potential to generate recurring income from the same customer, unless you publish multiple books over time.

When I was building my product, I decided to document my betting knowledge in the form of an e-book. This was the most sensible approach for me as I had a strategy that I had successfully implemented and wanted to be made available for everyone. I simply typed up everything I thought was relevant in a Microsoft Word document, formatted it, and converted it into a PDF file that I was ready to sell.

If you have useful knowledge that you want to share, an e-book may be the best route for you to take. For example, if you have an investment strategy that has made you money, a method to effectively train a pet dog, or a collection of tasty recipes, an e-book is a great way to document your knowledge in a format that can be easily understood and digested by your potential customers.

Video tutorials/guides: Similar to e-books, video tutorials are another method through which you can communicate and share your knowledge on a specific topic. Unlike e-books, video tutorials are tangible, engaging, and interactive which can be a lot more appealing for buyers. However, the time and cost involved with creating video tutorials are greater as compared to e-books.

If your niche is related to something visual or active, a video tutorial may be the best route for you to take. For example, if you have created an effective workout routine or have devised unique methods of hairstyling, documenting this in video form may be the most suitable option.

Email subscription services: Rather than selling a one-off product such as an e-book or video tutorial, an email subscription service involves on-going communication with your customer base. For example, if you are a successful forex (forex exchange/currency) trader, rather than documenting your secret formula to success in an e-book, you can choose to instead offer a subscription service whereby you send your customers daily suggestions on what trades to make, allowing them to copy your trades and benefit from the same returns that you achieve. The benefit of this approach is that you do not have to spend time documenting all your knowledge in an e-book. Additionally, rather than a one-off sale, you can earn an on-going income by charging your customers a daily/weekly/monthly/quarterly/yearly subscription fee to receive your daily forex trading guidance. The only downside of this approach is that you have an on-going commitment of interacting with your customers on a daily basis.

When building my product, in addition to documenting my knowledge in an e-book, I also decided it would be worthwhile to offer my customers the option to subscribe (on a monthly basis) to an email service, whereby I send them daily emails containing suggestions on which football matches to bet on. In addition to earning an income from one-off sales of my e-book, the email subscription service added a second recurring income stream.

If you have knowledge in something that is not static and tends to change overtime, creating an email subscription service may be the best route for you to take.

Bespoke/customized services: Similar to a subscription service, a bespoke or customized service is where you offer your customer base a service that you tailor to their needs. For example, if you are highly experienced at creating business plans, rather than writing an e-book about how to write business plans, you can instead choose to help customers write business plans based on their specific requirements. You can offer a service where by a customer provides you a small set of information from which you help them create a business plan. Customers tend to highly value this type of service as it is tailored to their needs and is not simply a generic transfer of knowledge that they need to interpret and apply.

Author's Advice: *Before creating your product/service, I highly recommend considering one (or a combination) of the four options described above. When selecting which type of product/service is most suitable, consider the following two questions:*

1. *What knowledge or information am I interested in sharing?*
2. *What is the most suitable format to for my customers to receive this information?*

If it is not clear to you which product/service type is most suitable, browse through the ClickBank marketplace to get an idea of the type of products/services competitors in your niche are currently offering. This will help you shape your own product/service and possibly even identify ways to differentiate your product/service from your competitors'.

Once you identify the type of product/service that is most suitable for your niche, spend some time creating it. If you feel like you do not have the necessary skills to write an e-book or create a video tutorial, consider outsourcing some of the work to experts.

When creating my product, due to my limited budget, I could not afford to have an expert create or design my e-book. In my efforts to find cheap ways to outsource parts of the product creation, I came across a website called Fiverr. In a nutshell, Fiverr is a platform where regular people offer their skills, talents, or services in exchange for a fee (starting at $5). Some examples of relevant services on offer are: article/e-book writing, logo design, web design, video creation, voice overs, SEO (search engine optimisation), etc. Fiverr can very quickly become your most useful source for help with creating your product/service as you can find all the skills you need for an extremely reasonable price. When creating my product, I used Fiverr to design my logo ($5), to record a 2 minute voice over ($15), and to create a promotional video ($20).

The best part about creating your product is that you can be as involved as you choose to be. I personally enjoy designing websites, branding products, creating logos, and writing e-books. If you do not have the skills or motivation to create your entire product/service, do not hesitate to outsource some of the effort. It will allow you to focus on what you are good at and will ultimately result in a more refined product/service for your customers.

Creating an Online Presence

Once you have finished creating your product/service, it's time to consider all the key elements that need to be addressed to successfully create an online presence for your product/service. As an absolute minimum requirement, you need the following things to begin selling a product/service via an affiliate marketing platform:

1. An account with an affiliate marketing platform (such as ClickBank)
2. A website for your product/service containing the following pages:
   a. A landing page (also known as a sales page or a pitch page)

b. A thank-you page (the page that the customer sees once they purchase your product/service)

Simply put, the two items above are all you require to actually begin selling a product/service online. If you are in a rush with getting a product to market and do not have a long term plan in place, you can go ahead with the 2 items above and can begin selling. However, to increase your chances of achieving your first $10,000 and to create a product/service that is sustainable and has growth potential, I would recommend obtaining the following:

1. An account with an affiliate marketing platform (such as ClickBank)
2. A website for your product/service containing the following pages:
    a. A landing page (also known as a sales page or a pitch page)
    b. A thank you page (the page that the customer sees once they purchase your product/service)
    c. A contact us page (a page containing your contact information for potential customers, affiliates, and/or business partners)
    d. An affiliates page (a page containing important information to attract affiliates to market your product/service)
    e. A cross-sell page (where relevant, a page that markets other similar products/services, earning you a commission for each sale)
3. An account with an email marketing platform (such as Constant Contact).

If you build the three items above as part of your product/service, it will ensure that you can begin selling, that you will attract affiliates, and that you will be able to leverage your product in the long run. To help make everything clearer, let's dive into each of the items into a bit more details.

1. An account with an affiliate marketing platform (such as ClickBank)

As previously mentioned ClickBank has served as my vehicle to success and been a very easy and simple platform to work with. Consequently, I highly recommend that you create an account with ClickBank as well and make them your platform of choice. Once you have this all set up, let's move on to creating your website.

2. A website for your product/service

Creating an appealing website for your product/service is a key piece in the $10,000 puzzle. Your website will serve as the gateway to your product (similar to a high street shop's window display) and consequently needs to communicate the right information in the right way.

First of all, you require a landing page. A landing page, essentially your home page, is the page on your website that affiliates will direct potential customers to. As a result, it is essential to include the following information on your landing page:

- Name and description of your product/service
- The sales pitch (why anyone should purchase your product/service)

- The benefits, performance, or differentiating factors of your product/service
- The cost of your product/service
- A call to action (e.g. a "Buy Now" button)

Author's Advice: *Once again, if you are not experienced in building websites or writing sales pitches, do not hesitate to outsource some of this work via platforms such as Fiverr. I also recommend visiting the sales pages of competing products in your niche. This will help you generate ideas on the kind of content you want or don't want on your landing page.*

Second, you need to create a thank you page. A thank you page is the page that your customers will be directed to once they purchase your product/service. This is simply a page that gives you the opportunity to provide any relevant information to new customers. For example, if your product is an e-book, it is common provide the instructions to download/access your e-book on the thank you page. If you run an email subscription service, the thank you page may contain instructions on how the new customer can join your mailing list.

Third, although this is not absolutely necessary, I recommend creating a contact us page. A contact us page very simply provides a method for anyone to contact you. This could be via a contact form or by simply listing your email address. The benefits of having a contact us page is that it gives potential customers and affiliates the opportunity to contact you if they have any questions. This could be the difference between you making a sale or losing a sale.

Fourth, although not mandatory, considering including an affiliate page. An affiliate page is a page dedicated to potential affiliates and is an opportunity for you to provide all the information an affiliate needs to effectively market your product. The more information you provide on your affiliate page, the more affiliates you are likely to attract as it will make it easier for affiliates to begin marketing your product. Considering including information such as:

- Sales figures and conversion rates (if available)
- Commission being offered
- Marketing material (banner ads, email marketing templates, product logos)
- Instructions on how the affiliate can create a personal hop-link (this information is readily available on ClickBank)

Fifth, although not absolutely required, consider including a cross-sell page. A cross-sell page is an opportunity for you to affiliate market other similar products that your potential customers are likely to be interested in. For example, let's say your product is an e-book on how to make money through forex trading. Your cross-sell page could include competing products on making money through commodities trading or index trading. The benefit of having a cross sell page is that even if a potential customer does not decide to purchase your product, they may visit your cross-sell page and choose to purchase one of the other similar products you have listed, for which you will receive an affiliate commission (more details in the "Becoming an Affiliate" section).

Author's Advice: *When creating a cross-sell page, ensure that the other products you choose to list are of high quality. In order to build a trusting and loyal customer base, it is essential that your recommendations are good recommendations. At the same time however,* *ensure that the products on your cross-sell page are of similar calibre to your product and not significantly better. Having products that are significantly better than yours on your cross-sell page devalues your product in the eyes on your potential customers.*

3. An account with an email marketing platform

The final piece in creating a strong online presence is to create an account with an email marketing platform such as Constant Contact. Constant Contact is a service that allows you to create and manage mailing lists so you can effectively communicate with your customers. A few of its key features are that it provides sign-up forms that you can add to your landing or thank you pages which allow customers to sign up to your mailing list and it allows you to create personalized follow up emails that can automatically be sent to all your subscribers. It also provides useful statistics on how many users click on your emails and the content within it, which helps assess and improve the effectiveness of your emails. This makes it easy for you to manage your customers and to effectively communicate with them. Additionally, if you are running an email subscription service, it will allow you to create emails and send them to all or subsets of your subscribers.

When I first launched my subscription service, I attempted to manually send emails to my subscribers. However, as the number of subscribers grew, this quickly became unmanageable. At that point, I signed up to Constant Contact, and haven't looked back since. It has significantly simplified the process of communicating with my subscribers and has highly automated the process by which new customers can sign up to my mailing list(s).

Author's Advice: To learn a bit more about email marketing platforms, visit Constant Contact's website for a high level overview of their features. In addition to the structure and convenience email marketing platforms offer, growing a targeted mailing list is one of the most important steps you will take in your journey to your first $10,000 (more on this in the "Become an Affiliate" chapter).

Before we move on to step 4, there is just one more item I'd like to quickly cover, costs. The costs involved with creating a product/service can vary based on your skillset and the amount of time you are willing to dedicate. When building my product/service, the costs were as follows:

- ClickBank one-time activation fee (only required for creators of products) - $49.95
- Website domain name and hosting services - $29.99
- Video and logo design (via Fiverr) – $40
- Constant Contact subscription – 60 day free trial, followed by around $20/month

Overall, I was able to create, design, and being selling my product/service for approximately $120 with the only on-going cost being my Constant Contact subscription. When designing your product/service, outsourcing lots of the work will mean that you save time in the process but will probably have a spent a bit more money (not significant if cheap outsourcing methods, such as Fiverr, are used). Alternatively, if you decide to build and design everything yourself, your costs could fall under $100. This is the beauty of the digital world. You can create and sell a product for close to nothing which is unheard of in traditional sales channels. Think about your skill set, your priorities, and your budget when making decisions on where and how to spend your money.

All in all, if you apply and incorporate all the suggestions provided in this section, the chances of creating a successful product and a strong online presence, will greatly improve. It is not uncommon for the majority of time to be spent on step 2, so be patient when putting together your product, and it will pay off in the long run.

Step 3: Marketing and Selling

Once you complete step two and have managed to create both a product and an online presence, the excitement and anticipation begins as it is time to prepare for sales. There are two key steps you need to take in order begin selling your product/service. First, you need to ensure that all the admin tasks have been completed and you have been setup and approved to sell on your chosen affiliate marketing platform. Second, you need to line up affiliates to market your product to increase exposure and drive traffic to your landing page. Let's examine these two steps in a bit more detail.

Configuring Your Product/Service for Sales

As mentioned previously, if you follow all the advice in step 2, you will have everything you require to begin selling your product on ClickBank. Once you have everything you need, it is about putting everything in place and switching everything on. Below is a list of the key steps you need to take to ensure ClickBank can process sales of your product/service. Further details on each of the steps below can be found here.

1. Ensure your landing page and thank you pages contain all the mandatory information required by ClickBank (or the affiliate marketing platform of your choice)
2. Ensure the call to action (payment link) on your landing page is set up as per ClickBank's standards (or the affiliate marketing platform of your choice)
3. Ensure you complete the "My Site" section of your ClickBank account to confirm your product/service is

listed in the ClickBank marketplace and is available for affiliates to begin marketing

4. Ensure you complete the "My Products" section of your ClickBank account to confirm all your products are set up and approved to sell at the price and commission of your choice.

Once you complete all of the steps above, your product/service will be ready and approved by ClickBank to begin selling.

Attracting Affiliates

Now that your product/service is listed on the ClickBank marketplace, affiliates will have visibility of it, and may or may not choose to market it based on the relevance and their perceived quality of the product/service. In order to improve the chances that affiliates will choose to market your product/service, consider the following approaches:

Marketplace Listing: When listing your product/service on ClickBank's marketplace (via the "My Site" section of your account), ensure that your product title and description are catchy and appealing for affiliates. Rather than focusing on what your product/service does, focus on the saleability of your product/service by highlighting statistics such as your generous commissions, your high conversion rates, and your low refund rates. These are the factors that affiliates considering when assessing whether to market a specific product. It is also worthwhile including the link to your affiliate page (if you created one) in your marketplace product description so that interested affiliates know exactly where to go to learn more about your product/service and to obtain all the tools/materials they require to begin marketing your product/service.

Make Friends: Once your product is listed on the marketplace, you can simply wait for affiliates to begin marketing it. This may or may not happen as it is hard to predict the appeal of your product. As a result, to help improve the chances of attracting affiliates, it is vital that you begin "making friends". Do some research online of how your competitors' products/services are being marketed online. Are there several articles being posted? Are there websites that review products? Are there discussion forums revolving around specific product categories? Based on the results of your research, start contacting the owners of these pages/forums/websites/blogs that have the ability to create buzz and drive traffic to your landing page. Provide them with a description of your product, the saleability, and the commission you are offering. This will bring your product to their attention and will increase the likelihood that your product will quickly get exposure.

Social Media: Marketing products and keeping followers engaged on social media can be a full-time job in itself. If you have time on your hands or already have a strong social media following, consider creating groups and/or pages on Facebook, posting promotional videos on YouTube, and sharing articles and/or blogposts about your product/service on Twitter to create additional buzz around your product. If it is of interest to people, your exposure can multiply as individuals share and engage with your content.

Author's Advice: *Of the approaches discussed above, making friends is by far the most important and can mean the difference between* *achieving your first $10,000 in a few weeks as opposed to a few years. When I was preparing my product/service for sales, I did a bit of research and discovered several popular websites that reviewed betting products to help their user bases make more informed decisions. I simply contacted some of the most popular ones and asked them to review my product/service. The benefit of doing this is that it gave me immediate exposure and created a buzz around my product/service as several articles and reviews were being published, and several users were interacting with the content by posting questions and comments. As a result of these reputable websites posting articles and reviews, I generated sales very quickly and the websites benefited from earning commissions from each sale (as affiliates).*

Step 4: Growing and Leveraging

Once you have built a product, created on online presence, and have been noticed by affiliates, the traffic will begin to roll in and you will begin to generate sales. The feeling you get when you make that first sale can be very liberating, so enjoy it while it lasts, as it can only happen once (per product ☺). Once you are done celebrating your first sale, it is time to focus on step 4 - ensuring that you make the most of all the traffic being directed to your landing page.

Not every person who lands on your product page will purchase your product. In fact, the majority of visitors will not purchase your product and will be likely to spend a very short time on your website. However, it is vital to not simply let them visit your website and leave with nothing. Similar to a traditional shop, all shop owners love to have customers visit their store and browse through their products. They very well know that not every customer will purchase something. However, every good shop owner ensures that they provide every customer (whether they purchase something or not) incentive to revisit the store or recommend it to someone else. Some traditional methods include handing out free samples, offering discount coupons, entering prize draws or providing brochures of upcoming product launches and/or events. Similarly, it is essential to capture information on EVERY customer that visits your website to increase the chances that they will revisit. As previously mentioned, having an email marketing service such as Constant Contact is essential as it provides you the opportunity to capture information about your visitors to help increase the chances that they will purchase either your product/service or a product/service that you recommend.

There are several different ways through which you can capture information on your visitors (with their consent), some of which are listed below:

Offer something for free: Offering something for free is a very common and effective way to gather information on the majority of your visitors. Most people that visit your website will not purchase your product. However, if you offer something relevant to your product for free, they are highly likely to take up that offer. Consider the type of product/service that you are selling and think of something that you can offer for free that won't take you much time or effort to create, but will add value for your visitors and increase the chances that they will purchase your product. For example, if you are selling an e-book, consider offering the first chapter of that e-book (or a preview of it) for free. This may very well help convince some potential customers to purchase your entire e-book. If you are providing a service, consider offering a few days of your service for free (e.g. a free trial). Once again, this can help convert potential customers into sales. For example, when I launched my service, I offered a few days of betting tips for free. As a result of this, I very quickly built a mailing list of individuals I knew were interested in betting. At the same time, if my tips during the free trial were successful, the chances that the individual would join the service as a paying customer significantly increased.

Offer something valuable: If you are not comfortable offering something for free, think of something else that you can offer which is of value to your target market. For example, if you are selling a guide on how to make money through forex trading, you can offer all of your visitors a history of your trades in the last 60 days, in exchange for their email address. The majority of them will be interested in this information as it will help them make a decision on whether to purchase your product. On the flip side, you will very quickly build a targeted mailing list of individuals who are interested in forex trading.

Offer an on-going commitment: If you do not have anything free or valuable to offer your visitors, consider sharing useful content on a regular basis as an incentive for your visitors to remain engaged. For example, if you are selling an e-book containing healthy 30-minute recipes, you can share a monthly newsletter containing tips on healthy cooking. Visitors who are interested in receiving this newsletter will subscribe to your mailing list.

Using all or a combination of the suggestions above will help you quickly build a mailing list of people who are extremely relevant to your niche. This is a goldmine of information which can help you grow very quickly and can create additional sources of income. If and when your first product/service is a success, you will naturally look to launch a second product/service. Your second product launch will be significantly easier as you already have "friends" in the industry to market your product and you yourself have built a mailing list that you can target for your new product launch. So to reiterate, make sure you offer EVERY visitor incentive to join one of your mailing lists as this will help you leverage and grow your current and future products.

Summary

Congratulations! You now have all the information and tools you require to make your first $10,000. I am very pleased you have reached this section of the book as having read through all the advice and guidance contained within the 4 steps clearly indicates that you are serious about achieving your first $10,000. I appreciate that it can seem like a lot of information to digest in a short space of time. Therefore, the following checklist should serve as a reminder of all the key points that were discussed and can provide you structure as you progress through your journey. Remember, all that stands between you and your first $10,000 is this:

1. **Idea Generation:**
    a. Spend some time reflecting on your interests and passions to help you identify a niche to target.
    b. Visit DMOZ or the ClickBank marketplace for further inspiration.
2. **Creation & Design:**
    a. **Create your product/service:**
        i. Agree the type of product you want to create (e-book, email subscription, etc.).
        ii. Decide which parts you want to build yourself and which parts you want to outsource (via Fiverr).
    b. **Create an online presence:**
        i. Create an account with an affiliate marketing platform like ClickBank
        ii. Create a website for your product/service like iPage

   iii. Create an account with an email marketing platform like Constant Contact

3. **Marketing & Selling:**
  a. Configure your product/service for sales
  b. Work on your marketplace listing, start making friends, and build a social media presence to effectively attract affiliates.

4. **Growing & Leveraging:**
  a. Offer incentive for EVERY visitor to subscribe to one of your mailing lists.

Author's Advice: *I recommend using the list above as a checklist to keep you on track towards achieving your first $10,000. All the information and the work involved can be overwhelming when read for the first time and in a short space of time. However, if you look at each step in isolation, there is nothing overly challenging or complicated in the process. Simply approach it one item at a time and progress through the steps at your own pace. Before you know it, you will be on your journey to your first $10,000 and it will feel completely natural.*

I wish you the best of luck!

Becoming an Affiliate

You now have all the information you require to earn your first $10,000 as product/service creator. Rather than stopping there, let's explore a second dimension that can help propel your income to new heights. As highlighted throughout the book, one of the key factors to succeeding as a product/service creator is your ability to create a product that is appealing for affiliates to market to their followers. Creating a product that does not appeal to affiliates can ultimately result in very few sales due to lack of endorsements and exposure.

The reason that affiliates are so powerful and influential is simply because they have access to targeted audiences in the form of mailing lists, followers, or subscribers. In most cases, they have spent lots of time and effort to build these followings through consistently providing valuable content or by creating and selling products/services of their own. Once you begin selling your product/service and begin building a mailing list, you too can start playing the role of an affiliate (in addition to that of a creator). Similar to affiliates, you now have access to a targeted audience in the form of a mailing list. As a result, you can visit the ClickBank marketplace and identify products/services that you believe will appeal to your audience.

The process of selecting suitable products/services to market to your audience is a sensitive one and should be approached carefully. I highly recommend following the guidelines below to ensure that you remain trustworthy and reputable in the eyes of your subscribers:

- Try or buy the product you plan to market before sharing it with your audience. It is very hard to truly devise whether a product is of high quality without trying it yourself. In many cases, you can simply contact the product owner and ask them to share it with you for free (which most of them will be willing to do for affiliates).
- Contact the product owner to obtain further information on the product/service and to get a feel for the level of customer support that is provided. Recommending a product run by a disorganized owner/team can very quickly damage your reputation in the eyes of your subscribers.
- Focus on products that are popular, that offer healthy commissions (50% or higher), and that exhibit healthy sales and conversion figures.
- Focus on subscription products with rebill and upsell opportunities. Products that offer rebills and upsells will help generate an on-going income rather than a one-off commission. For example, marketing an e-book to your audience may result in 50 sales for which you receive a one-off commission. However, generating the same 50 sales for a subscription service will mean that you receive an on-going commission every month that your referrals subscribe to that service versus just a one-off commission.
- Focus on products that are relevant to your niche. Let's say you created an e-book containing Mexican food recipes and built up a mailing list of 1000 people. It would be sensible for you to market high quality products relevant to cooking, such as recipe books in other cuisines or products on nutrition.

Marketing irrelevant products such as betting systems or investment books to your audience will result in very few sales (if any) and will cause lots of them unsubscribing as the information you are sending them is irrelevant to their needs.

Author's Advice: *Following the guidelines discussed above will ensure that your mailing list remains loyal and continues to trust your recommendations and judgement. As soon as you start recommend low quality products/services, your audience will lose faith in your judgement and your mailing list, which you would have spent lots of time and effort in building up, will quickly lose value. Cherish your mailing list and treat your subscribers with the respect they deserve. In return, you are far more likely to earn lots of money in the form of affiliate commissions from your loyal following.*

Useful Tools and Links

Through my experience of creating and selling digital products/services online, I've come across several tools and services which have helped simplify my journey to my first $10,000. Here are some of the services I recommend (some of which have already been mentioned):

ClickBank: ClickBank was my chosen affiliate marketing platform which has served me very well through my journey. In order to make the most of the advice in this book, I highly recommend using ClickBank as your affiliate marketing platform as well (although a lot of the advice/guidance is applicable across the industry).

iPage: When building a website for my product/service, I used iPage to purchase my domain, host my website, and to build my website. iPage offers pre-set themes and drag-and-drop builders which makes building a website extremely easy and non-technical. Additionally, they also provide a webmail platform which allows you to access email accounts that you can create using your domain name (e.g. name@yourdomainname.com).

Constant Contact: In order to effectively run a subscription service, an email marketing service like Constant Contact is essential. Additionally, it is also necessary if you want to build a mailing list to further grow and leverage your products/services. Constant Contact is very easy to use and has served me well. The following website summarises Constant Contact's feature set.

Fiverr: When building my product and website, I wanted to outsource certain parts of the process as I didn't have the required skills to execute them effectively. Fiverr became my go to place to get anything done at a reasonable price, from logo design, to video creation, to SEO.

Disclaimer

All materials on this site may not be copied, modified, transmitted, translated, or otherwise distributed by any means without permission from myfirst10000.com.

myfirst10000.com is not necessarily affiliated with sites that may be linked in this site and is not responsible for their content. The linked sites are for your convenience only and you access them at your own risk.

The material on the myfirst10000.com website are provided "as is" and without warranties of any kind. Myfirst10000.com disclaims all warranties, express or implied, including, but not limited to, implied warranties of merchantability and fitness for a particular purpose. Myfirst10000.com does not warrant that the functions contained in the materials will be uninterrupted or error-free, that defects will be corrected, or that the myfirst10000.com website or the server that makes them available are free of viruses or other harmful components. Myfirst10000.com does not warrant or make any representations regarding the use or the results of the use of the materials in the myfirst10000.com website in terms of their correctness, accuracy, reliability, or otherwise. You (and not myfirst10000.com) assume the entire cost of all necessary servicing, repair or correction. Under no circumstances shall myfirst10000.com be liable for any special or consequential damages that result from the use of, or the inability to use, the materials in this site.

If you do not agree to the Terms of Use, discontinue using the site immediately.

Income Disclaimer

Any Earnings Or Income Statements Or Income Examples Or Sample Results Or Expected Earnings Figures/Statistics Are Only Estimates Of What We Think You Could Earn. There Is No Assurance You Will Do As Well As The Estimates. If You Rely Upon Our Figures; You Must Accept The Risk Of Possibly Not Doing As Well.

Any And All Claims Or Representations, As To Income Earnings On This Web Site, Are Not To Be Considered As Guaranteed Earnings.

There Can Be No Assurance That Any Prior Successes, Or Past Results, As To Income Earnings Or Win/Strike Rates, Can Be Used As An Indication Of Your Future Success Or Results.

Monetary Income And Traffic Results Are Based On Many Factors. We Have No Way Of Knowing How Well You Will Do, As We Do Not Know You, Your Background, Your Work Ethic, Or Your Business Skills Or Practices. Therefore We Do Not Guarantee Or Imply That You Will Win Any Incentives Or Prizes That May Be Offered, Get Rich, That You Will Do As Well, Or Make Any Money At All.

Internet Businesses And Earnings Derived There From, Have Unknown Risks Involved, And Are Not Suitable For Everyone. Making Decisions Based On Any Information Presented In Our Products, Services, Or Web Site, Should Be Done Only With The Knowledge That You Could Experience Significant Losses, Or Make No Money At All.

All Products And Services By Our Company Are For Educational And Informational Purposes Only. Use Caution And Seek The Advice Of Qualified Professionals. Check With Your Accountant, Lawyer Or Professional Advisor, Before Acting On This Or Any Information.

Users Of Our Products, Services And Web Site Are Advised To Do Their Own Due Diligence When It Comes To Making Business Decisions And All Information, Products, And Services That Have Been Provided Should Be Independently Verified By Your Own Qualified Professionals.

Our Information, Products, And Services On This Web Site Should Be Carefully Considered And Evaluated, Before Reaching A Business Decision, On Whether To Rely On Them. All Disclosures And Disclaimers Made Herein Or On Our Site, Apply Equally To Any Offers, Prizes, Or Incentives, That May Be Made By Our Company.

You Agree That Our Company Is Not Responsible For The Success Or Failure Of Your Decisions Relating To Any Information

Presented By Our Company, Or Our Company Products Or Services.

Privacy Policy

We maintain this page to demonstrate our firm commitment to the rights and privacy of our users. This page explains how our site collects information from our members.

Free Chapters Offer: we respect the privacy of our users, and as such we will never share our database of email addresses and names with any third party.

Upon confirmation that you would like to preview our product, we will from time to time send you free information relating to the products we market, general advice related to online marketing, and promotional material for other products. Your email will never be passed onto any third party. We will also never spam you. You may unsubscribe from the mailing list at any time.

Personal Information we collect and how it is used: Service provider: when you purchase and/or subscribe to My First $10,000, the payment is processed by Clickbank.com, who will collect your name, address, and credit card information so as to verify your order. They will not use the information for any other purpose. Upon ordering, we also collect your name and e-mail address. We use this information to follow-up on your order. We will not share leads with any other party and we do not sell our leads to any other party.

Revisions to This Policy: We reserve the right to revise, amend, or modify our policies and terms at any time and in any manner, by updating this page.

Click the following link for more information on ClickBank's Privacy Policy.

www.ingramcontent.com/pod-product-compliance
Lightning Source LLC
Chambersburg PA
CBHW071003180526
45168CB00003B/1264